M000248597

Monuments
Help Us Remember

Monuments Help Us Remember

a building block book

Lee Sullivan Hill

Carolrhoda Books, Inc./Minneapolis

Can a book be a monument? This book is for my grandmother Marjory Doherty Sullivan, may she rest in peace.—L. S. H.

For metric conversion, when you know the number of feet, multiply by 0.30 to find the number of meters.

The photographs in this book are reproduced through the courtesy of: **Tony Stone Images:** (© Tom Till) front cover, (© Chuck Pefley) p. 9, (© David Ball) p. 27; **TRIP:** (© B. Turner) back cover, p. 17, (© A. Tovy) p. 6, (© R. Surman) p. 7, (© W. Jacobs) p. 13, (© C. Rennie) p. 16, (© T. Why) p. 20, (© J. Greenberg) p. 26, (© P. Kaplan) p. 29; © Robert Fried/Robert Fried Photography, pp. 1, 10; © James P. Rowan, pp. 2, 5, 15, 22; © Donna Carroll/Travel Stock, p. 8; © Brian Spurlock/SportsChrome USA, p. 11; © Betty Crowell, pp. 12, 18, 28; © Buddy Mays/Travel Stock, pp. 14, 19; © CORBIS/Todd Gipstein, p. 21; © Howard Ande, p. 23; © CORBIS/Bettmann, p. 25; © AP/Wide World Photos, p. 24.

Text copyright © 2001 by Lee Sullivan Hill

Carolrhoda Books, Inc.
A division of Lerner Publishing Group
241 First Avenue North
Minneapolis, Minnesota 55401 U.S.A.

Website address: www.lernerbooks.com

Library of Congress Cataloging-in-Publication Data

Hill, Lee Sullivan, 1958–
    Monuments help us remember / Lee Sullivan Hill.
        p. cm.—(A building block book)
    Summary: Describes different kinds of monuments from around the world while also explaining how and why they were built, how they are preserved, and their importance to one's memory.
    ISBN 1-57505-475-2 (lib. bdg : alk paper)
    1. Monuments—Juvenile literature. 2. Memory—Social aspects—Juvenile literature. 3. Memory—Political aspects—Juvenile literature. [1. Monuments 2. Memory.] I. Title. II. Series: Hill, Lee Sullivan, 1958– Building block book.
CC135. H55 2001
725'.94—dc21   99-050606

Manufactured in the United States of America
1 2 3 4 5 6 – JR – 06 05 04 03 02 01

Monuments stand solid and strong for ages.
They hold memories for people and communities
all around the world.

Do you save treasures to remember special times? Smooth rocks from the beach remind you of the summer. Photographs remind you of a trip you took.

Monuments are like your photos and treasures. They remind us of events that changed history. They help us remember people who made a difference.

For thousands of years, people have built monuments to honor great leaders. Ancient Egyptians carved giant statues of their pharaohs and queens.

Americans have built many monuments to George Washington. He led the armies that fought for freedom from Britain. After the Revolutionary War, Americans asked him to be their first president.

Some monuments honor citizens who helped their communities. In the 1500s, Beatriz Hernández led 64 families through the mountains. She promised to protect their new home in Guadalajara, Mexico.

Michael Jordan made everyone feel like a winner. The monument to Michael makes a slam dunk in Chicago. You can almost hear the crowd cheer.

Some monuments remind us of tall tales from
the past. Paul Bunyan and his blue ox, Babe,
greet visitors to California's Redwood Forest.

A loyal dog named Bobby watches over the
town of Edinburgh, Scotland. Monuments like
this one honor pets that people have loved.

Many monuments help us remember events in history. The French people were proud of battles won by their army in the 1800s. They built a huge arch in Paris, their capital city.

Independence Monument in Kenya reaches to the sky. It celebrates the African nation's freedom from British rule in 1963.

Sometimes people build monuments to
remember sad events. During World War II, an
atomic bomb killed thousands of Japanese
citizens in the city of Hiroshima. A monument in
Japan reminds us to learn from the past.

Other monuments inspire us to dream of the future. Russians built the Space Monument after a man flew to outer space for the first time. Where will space travel take us next?

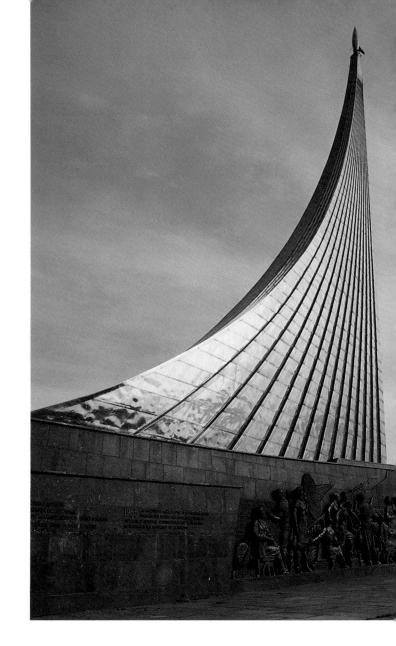

Monuments to people and events take many
different forms: statues, arches, towers—even
palaces. An Indian emperor built the Taj Mahal
to remember his wife after she died.

A simple headstone honors a loved one who died. Sarah may not have been famous, but she was important to her family.

A long, black wall helps us remember, too.
Carved into the monument's smooth stone are
thousands of names. The Wall honors the
American soldiers killed in the Vietnam War.

A waterfall reminds us of Dr. Martin Luther King, Jr., and the struggle for civil rights. The monument honors people who fought for fairness for all races.

Some monuments invite you to come inside. Ride to the top of the Gateway Arch. Imagine thousands of covered wagons setting out on the Oregon Trail in the 1800s. Pioneers began their journey right here in Saint Louis, Missouri.

Climb up to the top of a tall monument. Inside, it is dark and shady. But look outside the window. The bright sun makes a shadow on the ground below. Whose shadow could it be?

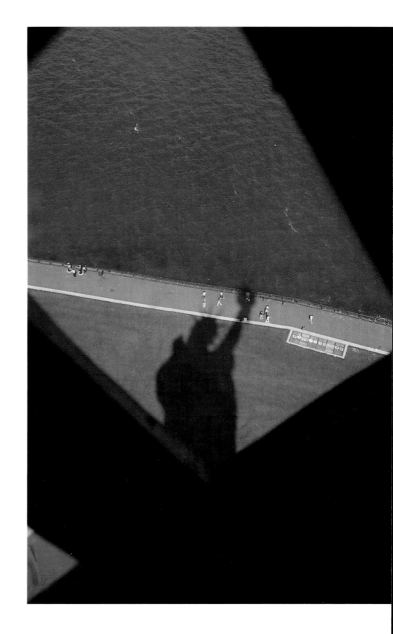

Monuments that last for ages take years to plan and build. First, people in a community decide what kind of monument they want. They ask sculptors to draw pictures of different ideas. Then they choose one sculptor to work on the monument.

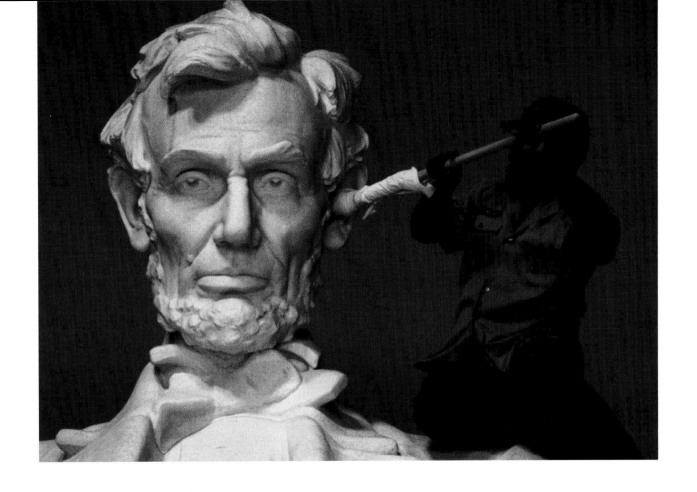

More work remains after monuments are built. They need to be cleaned and protected. Wind, rain, and air pollution damage stone and metal. Without care, monuments would crumble.

Next time you visit a monument, think about people who lived in the past. Close your eyes for a moment and wonder.

When you grow up, you could be a sculptor and create famous monuments. Or you could travel the wide world over and see history cast in stone.

Monuments hold memories for millions of
people. They celebrate the people and events that
changed our world.

Across the ages, monuments help us remember.

A Photo Index to the Monuments in This Book

Cover The Statue of Liberty greets visitors to New York Harbor. France gave Lady Liberty to the United States in 1884 as a symbol of friendship.

Page 1 A statue in the Marais district of Paris stands as a reminder of the past. This section of Paris was once one of the most powerful and fashionable neighborhoods in all of France.

Page 2 The Washington Monument towers over Washington, D.C. The first limestone block was laid in 1848, but the monument wasn't completed until 1884.

Page 5 This unusual monument in Campeche, Mexico, seems to rise right out of the ground. The stone sculpture is known as "The Resurgence of Campeche."

Page 6 A photo taken in front of the Bear and Madrona statue brings back happy memories of Madrid, Spain. What treasures do you keep to remember special times?

Page 7 Forty-six years after President Abraham Lincoln's death, the United States Congress voted to honor him with a monument. Daniel Chester French carved this statue, which sits inside a Greek-style temple designed by Henry Bacon.

Page 8 These statues of Ramses II and his wife, Queen Nefertari, have guarded the entrance to the temple at Abu Simbel in Egypt for more than three thousand years.

Page 9 A bronze statue of George Washington stands in the Boston Public Gardens. Sculptors often use bronze because the metal, which is made from a mixture of copper and tin, does not rust easily.

Page 10 This statue of Beatriz Hernández stands in the Historic District of Guadalajara, Mexico. It is another example of a bronze monument. To learn how bronze monuments are made, read *Shaping a President: Sculpting for the Roosevelt Memorial*, by Kelli Peduzzi and photographer Diane Smook.

 **Page 11** This statue of basketball star Michael Jordan was built in 1994. The bronze form stands 12 feet tall and weighs 2,000 pounds.

 Page 12 Paul Bunyan and his blue ox, Babe, come alive in this monument in Klamath, California.

 **Page 13** A skye terrier remembered as Greyfriar's Bobby guarded his master's grave for fourteen years. After Bobby died, this statue was built to remember the dog's loyalty.

 **Page 14** In the early 1800s, French emperor Napoleon I hired an architect to design the Arc de Triomphe. Sculptors carved battle scenes into panels that decorate the 164-foot-tall arch.

 **Page 15** The Independence Monument was built in 1963 to celebrate the founding of the Republic of Kenya. It stands in the capital city, Nairobi.

 **Page 16** The Cenotaph in Hiroshima, Japan, contains the names of the people killed by the atomic bomb during WWII.

 **Page 17** The monument "To the Conquerors of Space" was built in 1964. It celebrates the launching of *Sputnik.* It also honors the scientists and engineers who made space travel possible.

 **Page 18** Shah Jahan built the Taj Mahal in Agra, India, in the 1600s. It is said that he built the palace to honor his wife. But some researchers believe Shah Jahan may have built the palace for himself.

 **Page 19** Gravestones like this one in New Harmony, Indiana, mark the place where a person is buried. Stone markers help families remember their loved ones who have died.

 **Page 20** The Vietnam War Veterans Memorial is in Washington, D.C. The black granite wall is set low in the ground. Visitors walk down a ramp to read the names.

 **Page 21** The Civil Rights Memorial in Montgomery, Alabama, is also carved from smooth, black granite. Sculptor Maya Lin designed both this monument and the Vietnam War Veterans Memorial.

 **Page 22** Trams carry visitors to the top of this 630-foot-tall steel arch in Saint Louis, Missouri. It is called the Gateway Arch because of the city's nickname—Gateway to the West.

 **Page 23** Do you know whose shadow this is? Here's a clue: look at the cover of this book. Notice the torch held high. Now can you guess? It's the Statue of Liberty's shadow.

 **Page 24** Sculptor Ed Dwight works on a monument he designed. In 1999, the State Assembly in South Carolina chose Mr. Dwight to create an African American Memorial for the State House.

 **Page 25** A worker cleans the Lincoln Memorial with a giant swab. Scientists and museum conservators are working together to invent coatings to protect monuments from decay.

 **Page 26** These visitors to the Bunker Hill Monument in Charlestown, Massachusetts, are learning about the first big clash between American and British soldiers in the Revolutionary War.

 **Page 27** The Mount Rushmore National Memorial is located in the Black Hills of South Dakota. The monument to presidents George Washington, Thomas Jefferson, Theodore Roosevelt, and Abraham Lincoln draws visitors from around the world.

 **Page 28** The United States Congress voted in 1986 to create a Korean War Veterans Memorial in Washington, D.C. The squad of 19 stainless steel soldiers was created by sculptor Frank Gaylord.

 **Page 29** The Thomas Jefferson Memorial was dedicated on April 13, 1943, 200 years after Jefferson's birth. Jefferson drafted the Declaration of Independence and was the third president of the United States.